S E X

How to Talk to Your Partner About Sex

Jake Dunn

INTRODUCTION

Now and again it can feel troublesome; yet conversing with your accomplice about sex is an interest in your relationship. Here are ways for talking successfully:

a. Plan time ahead to discuss sex. By putting this discussion on your plan, you kill the likelihood that this discussion will emerge out of anger or frustration.

b. Talk about what's working and so forth. Numerous issues that couples insight in the room can be corrected by working them out. Find ways to compromise so you both have a good sense of security and heard.

c. Make ideas for your accomplice about what you would like. Positive ideas frequently work better as opposed to whining about the things they're now doing or not doing.

d. Speak the truth about what you need. Be that as it may, don't talk your accomplice into anything they're not happy trying. Likewise don't permit your accomplice to do same to you.

e. Be available to one another's thoughts. Think twice about them, as well, so that both of you feel appreciated and get what you really want.

f. Be clear and genuine. This will forestall less space for miscommunication. Try not to cause your accomplice to need to find out a deeper, hidden meaning. On the off chance that you need something yet are awkward expressing it, try writing it down instead.

Issues with sex and sexual fulfillment can cause relationship and conjugal pain. Despite the fact that it is a typical issue, discussing sex with your accomplice can dismay. Offering issues to outsiders online could feel simpler for you than examining them straightforwardly with your accomplice, which could make sense of why sex is so generally talked about in online relationship forums.

These discussions can deliver critical tension, which can make you keep away from them by and large. Realizing a couple of systems can make them simpler, nonetheless, and you're probably going to find "the sex talk" worth the work.

CHAPTER 1

Motivations to Discuss Sex with Your Accomplice

Research has found that couples who have solid sexual communication are happier with their sex lives. Assuming that you're encountering issues with your sex life, discussing them with your accomplice could further develop your sex life and your relationship.

Open communication can prompt more noteworthy sensations of closeness and a more grounded relationship. As a matter of fact, talking genuinely with your accomplice could build your general fulfillment in your relationship.

Key Topics to Talk About

Sex-related topics you ought to discuss with your accomplice could include:

- Change in charisma
- Want to have a go at a new thing
- Family planning

- o Sensations of sexual rejection or continuously having to start sex
- o Absence of closeness or the need for more love
- o Absence of sexual fulfillment
- o Sexual brokenness

Discussing Safe Sex

Rehearsing safe sex is vital, particularly assuming your relationship is available to other people. Inquire as to whether they've utilized condoms and other security measures while drawing in with other sexual accomplices. In like manner, speak the truth about your own practices. In the event that either of you haven't practiced safe sex, talk about fitting testing for all involved parties.

Between selective accomplices in a monogamous relationship, raising this issue can be particularly troublesome in the event that it brings up issues of fidelity. On the off chance that you have participated in any sort of sexual movement with another person or suspect that your accomplice has, it's the ideal opportunity for a blunt, if troublesome, discussion and testing.

Discussing Your Cravings

Your solace level is a significant piece of having a fantastic sexual coexistence. Your accomplice can't guess what you might be thinking, so letting them know what you need can improve the sexual experience for both of you. Examine what causes you to feel stirred and wanted. On the off chance that your accomplice is missing the mark regarding your assumptions, convey this tenderly and valuably, and give suggestions you think could help.

Take a stab at discussing your sexual dreams. This may be troublesome at first but remember that everybody has them, and they will more often than not fall into a couple of normal classifications. Being vulnerable in this manner can build closeness between you and your accomplice and could try and prompt a few groundbreaking thoughts for sexual activities.

At the point when you don't Need Sex

Drive can change over time, and once in a while, two individuals essentially don't adjust in that frame of mind of sexual craving. At the point when you would prefer not to engage, make sure to speak with your accomplice sincerely and delicately.

If low or jumbled charisma is a common issue that is creating issues in your relationship, consider consulting a healthcare provider or counselor for advice. There are numerous factors to consider with regard to sex drive including your physical and psychological well-being.

When to Discuss Sex

There is a general setting to examine sex with your accomplice. Waiting for the right moment to address the subject can assist you with getting around a portion of those sensations of distress or clumsiness that can be normal during sex talks. You ought to likewise:

Pick an unbiased area. Try not to discuss sexual issues in your room or at sleep time. Pick an unbiased area that is private and agreeable for both of you.

Keep away from post-sex talks. Try not to discuss sex-related issues just in the wake of having intercourse. Sit tight for when you can be more objective and eliminated from the current topic.

Try not to catch off-guard your accomplice. If you have any desire to discuss sexual issues, let your accomplice know (without finding fault) that you think you two need to talk. Put down a point in time and a spot, and contemplate what you might want to examine in advance.

How to Discuss Sex with Your Accomplice

Here are a few methodologies for making discussions about sex simpler for both of you.

Begin Gradually

Have a "delicate beginning" to the discussion. Start with your objective to feel nearer and associated with your accomplice. Abstain from accusing. Skip analysis, and spotlight on things you both can do to make your sex life seriously satisfying.

Center around Closeness

Recall that warmth and closeness are similarly all around as significant as recurrence. Investigate ways of building closeness and feel more connected past intercourse, and discuss your requirements for different sorts of love and consideration, as well.

Avoid the Astonishments

You should both be in total agreement, so start these discussions prior to unveiling any astonishment to your accomplice. Discuss what you both could appreciate and the dreams you have. On the off chance that you truly do choose to bring a portion of these into your relationship, research your choices together.

To try not to make issues in your sexual coexistence, don't buy sex guidance books or sex toys without discussing the issue with your accomplice first.

Communicate your thoughts

Chat with each other about expectations, fears, wants, and concerns — and tell the truth. Share your deepest contemplations and sentiments with respect to your sexual relationship, and assist your partner with having a good sense of security enough to do likewise.

Talk Frequently

The "sex talk" is certainly not a one-time discussion; it ought to be a continuous conversation and a typical piece of your relationship. Needs and wants can change over time. Check-in with your accomplice frequently.

How to Have Troublesome Discussions About Your Marriage

Grasp Your Sexual Style

Realizing your sexual style can assist you with understanding which types of closeness you view as the most fulfilling — and similar sounds accurate for your accomplice. Investigate your sexual styles with each other. All couples have these styles or temperaments at some point.

a. **Profound**: This is an association of the whole self that mirrors your profound enthusiasm for being with each other. Seeing the little minutes in your lives can upgrade your otherworldly association.

b. **Entertaining**: Chuckling and prodding each other in bed is tied in with having a good time together. There is a light and energetic undercurrent.

c. **Furious**: Having intercourse in any event, when you're ticked off at one another can recuperate.

Be that as it may, make certain to ultimately resolve the issues.

d. **Healthy**: This style is evil and coquettish. You could give each other enchanting looks or have speedy sex in an uncommon setting. This is about the delight and rawness of engaging in sexual relations.

e. **Delicate**: This style is the delicate, heartfelt, mending sex that might include rubs, light contact, and tending to each other. You both are into the actual sensations and spotlight on giving each other delight.

f. **Dream**: With this style, you two team up to be daring and experiment a bit. On the off chance that you integrate your dreams into sexual activity with your accomplice, put forth rules and honor each other's limits.

Assuming you and your accomplice have different sexual styles, transparent communication can help. Talking through your disparities can help you comprehend and address the distinctions, guaranteeing that you both feel fulfilled. You and your accomplice could likewise think about sex treatment assuming you want assistance.

Good lovers are made, not born, as the colloquialism goes. Assuming you really maintain that your sexual relationship should be everything that it could be set aside time to converse with each other.

Participating in regular communication is a significant part of any extraordinary relationship — and that incorporates discussing sex. This discussion is important for all couples, and it's anything but a one-time occasion. It's something you and your accomplice ought to participate in routinely from the outset of your relationship. Solid sexual coexistence is an extraordinary gift, and it's to be delighted in and supported.

Why Sex Is Significant for Most Connections

Frequently Asked Questions

<u>How would you converse with your accomplice about pain during sex?</u>

In the event that you're encountering dyspareunia (pain during sex), don't experience it peacefully. Tell the truth and open up with your accomplice. Look for clinical assistance to decide the reason.

Your solace is significant, and a decent sexual accomplice ought to be understanding and supportive.

<u>How would you discuss sex without it being off-kilter?</u>

The more habitually you talk about sex with your accomplice, the less off-kilter it will be. Recall that your accomplice can't guess what you might be thinking and may be feeling better when you express what's on yours. Pick a nonpartisan spot liberated from interruption and interference, and keep away from criticism.

<u>How would you discuss sex issues with your accomplice?</u>

Move towards it as you would some other issue in your relationship. Be delicate to your accomplice's sentiments and keep away from criticism. Pick a nonpartisan spot and when you will not be interfered with so both of you have a real sense of security and can be pretty much as open as could be expected. Couples' treatment can likewise give a place of refuge to discuss sexual issues.

<u>How would you discuss sex with a potential marriage accomplice?</u>

On the off chance that your accomplice appears to be keen on marriage, it's critical to talk about assumptions about sex. It's a major part of a sound marriage for a great many people, and knowing what's essential to your accomplice can build closeness. Begin gradually, pick an unbiased spot where you will not be interfered with, and be delicate to your accomplice's sentiments. You may likewise decide to attempt pre-marital counseling, which can be a protected, supportive spot to examine sex for certain couples.

Discussing sex is an expertise

From ways of behaving to announcements, ideas of sex and sexuality channel into our lives. However, having the jargon for sex doesn't necessarily in every case make an interpretation so flawlessly into agreeable discussions.

This is particularly obvious when it's about what we need from, and even during sex.

However, communication is important for having great sex. The readiness to discuss the sort of sex we have or need to have is key expertise.

When you keep away from those essential discussions, you could stay away from some cumbersomeness, but on the other hand you're making do with sub-par sex."

By having these discussions, you and your accomplice's relationship can have profound, psychological, and mental advantages.

CHAPTER 2

What We Discuss When We Discuss Sex

Private discussions aren't just about delight. Different topics about sex can include:

- o Sexual wellbeing
- o How habitually we'd like sex
- o The most effective method to explore unknowns
- o The most effective method to manage contrasts in what we and our accomplices appreciate

Discussing these points can likewise assist with building an establishment for a superior relationship as you find out about one another and investigate new things together, all while being in total agreement.

It's additionally worth moving beyond the inconvenience to discuss wellbeing, especially sexually transmitted infections (STIs) and contraception. Keeping away from these fundamental discussions may be jeopardizing your well-being and alter the future you'd expected.

More secure sex and anti-conception medication

The obligation of conception prevention has generally tumbled to individuals with a vagina, and that has been excessive weight. All accomplices should know about and engage with getting to and mindfully utilizing compelling techniques for conception prevention.

Condoms and other boundary techniques will give some security against transmission and can assist with forestalling pregnancy when utilized appropriately.

In the event that you have a relationship where you and your accomplice have decided to not utilize or quit utilizing condoms or other boundary techniques, you ought to begin one more discussion about conception prevention.

Anti-conception medication is the obligation of all interested parties. You and your accomplice share the experience, whether it's anti-conception medication side effects or pregnancy.

So why not ensure the outcome is what you both needed and anticipated?

There is a wide range of kinds of contraception, so make certain to converse with your doctor about what your choices are and what choice might be ideal for you.

How might you discuss how much sex you might want to have?

Each sound sexual relationship requires steady communication. Zeroing in on both your needs and the necessities of your partner is significant.

It's really smart to be open about what your needs are and to constantly keep the communication open.

To request less sex, you could have a go at underlining their attributes to recommend new ideas. Appeal to your accomplice's interests and structure another activity or date around it that both of you will appreciate.

Requesting pretty much or less sex can raise vulnerabilities.

Sexual inclinations ought to be not difficult to discuss on the grounds that they eventually lead to your pleasure, yet they're frequently challenging to talk about in light of the fact that we dread judgment.

Certain individuals would rather not be seen as too sexual in light of the fact that they need more sex. Others could stress that requesting less sex could infer that their accomplice isn't doing something right.

Integrate your concerns about yourself into the conversation. Discussing sex works best as a two-way discussion.

Consciously finding different preferences

Discussing how touches, subtleties, and even dreams of sex could advance is less clear than discussing STIs, anti-conception medication, or recurrence of sex.

Sexual preferences can run on a range. There are exercises that you love, ones you couldn't in fact contemplate, and those in between.

Also, what befalls things that you haven't as yet even known about? Or then again when do your longings change?

Conveying such private necessities requires an elevated degree of certainty and trust. Simultaneously, communication fabricates that certainty and trust.

Ponder what you would be OK with and what things you would be awkward with. Recall you can continuously adjust your perspective. Discussing these things with your accomplice assists keep things open.

Converse with a healthcare provider if you're concerned something you have any desire to attempt could be sexually or physically risky.

Starting up the discussion

Now and then we're hampered by an absence of language.

One of the obstructions for communication is that the language is either truly ridiculous sounding or clinical.

It's useful to begin in the viewpoint of pleasure and affection. Two accomplices who are sexually engaged with each other at last need to pleasure one another.

Use motion pictures to begin discussions and explore

Think about taking advantage of sexual feeling from entertainment, on the off chance that you actually can't carve out the words or opportunity to express whatever you might be thinking.

Watching motion pictures is an extraordinary method to facilitate discussions with your accomplice.

"For instance, assuming you might want to add a touch of a crimp in your room, a simple method for carrying it up with your accomplice is to watch a film together that highlights it."

Pose inquiries to get a feeling of how your accomplice might feel about it. At any point you can inquire, "Did you think that was hot?" or "could you have a go at something like that?'"

The spirit of discussions like these ought to be transparency and interest, not judgment.

"Assuming somebody unveils that they find something truly hot that you see as truly yucky, don't go, 'That is revolting!' This is a delicate area that ought to be explored tenderly."

Sexual entertainment gives a lot of motivation for hot suggestions.

It's completely fine not to proceed with anything you're awkward with.

CHAPTER 3

Where and When to Talk Sex

As well as getting the words properly aligned, relationship specialists bring up that where and when you have close discussions is significant.

Try not to talk sex when

a. they stroll into the entryway
b. they're eager or tired
c. in bed or before sleep time
d. previously or after sex

Discussing sex after sex might seem to be censuring or criticizing. Talking ahead of time could get you unsettled about conveying just precisely the exact thing your accomplice needs.

At the point when everything looks good, giving your accomplice a heads-up that your point may be somewhat strange.

Communications fundamentals

Regard and feeling regarded are key parts of a relationship.

Utilizing purported I-statements is a communication procedure that underscores the speaker's insight, without disgracing, accusing, or whining about the other individual.

A few models:

- o "I notice we are by all accounts having less foreplay before we making love. Could we at any point discuss ways of investing more energy in foreplay first?"
- o "I truly loved it when you were on top of me. Is there anything I can do to get a greater amount of that?"

How to explore differences

Assuming that regard is present, you can bridge gaps. However, at times it's shockingly difficult to be aware if that regard is there, particularly right off the early stage in a relationship.

Assuming that your new accomplice declines to get tested for STIs or to share their results, they might be nonverbally showing you their lack of regard. It's difficult to say if that particular situation will improve with time.

Yet, contrasts shouldn't bring about a final order. Separating isn't necessary when you and your long-term accomplice have contention in interests.

For instance, suppose I want to live in New York, and my accomplice needs to live in L.A. The solution is by no means to compromise and live in Kansas. No shade to Kansas, however, the two of us will forfeit bliss.

All things being equal, we both talk about what draws us in an area. I might require a city with lots of nightlife and galleries. My accomplice needs a spot close to the sea with a worldwide populace. The genuine solution may be Miami.

A cross-country move is somewhat more strategically convoluted than discussing sex. Be that as it may, both offer a similar key focal point: Figure out how to compromise to find bliss together.

Furthermore, you get to know somebody you care about a smidgen all the more profoundly, as well as yourself.

CHAPTER 4

How to Have a Blissful Sexual Coexistence

What is a blissful sexual coexistence?

Whether you've been in your relationship for 20 days or 20 years, you might have worries about your sexual coexistence as a couple.

Having a cheerful sexual coexistence has been connected to all that from better heart wellbeing to better relationship wellbeing. Yet, what is a blissful sexual coexistence?

Certain individuals accept a decent sexual coexistence depends on how frequently you two have intercourse. Others accept different or common climaxing is the key.

In truth, these things are not generally imperative to blissful sexual coexistence.

There's no enchanted number with regards to amount. What makes a difference is that each accomplice has a solid sense of security and agreeable, and they're having pleasurable sex.

What's important is a couple's capacity to speak with one another about the kind of sex they need to have.

How about we take a gander at approaches to further developing your sexual coexistence together, and how that may likewise work on improving your relationship.

Blissful sex tips

Further developing your sexual coexistence takes work and planning. In spite of prevalent thinking, this doesn't cause the romance to be removed from it. As a matter of fact, dealing with your sexual coexistence together can be an effective method for returning the romance back into your relationship.

Try not to clutch outrage

Outrage is a normal part of life. Now and again individuals even have furious sex. In any case, unmanaged outrage can crush sexual craving, trust, and connectivity. It very well may be difficult to feel delicate, adoring, or sexual toward somebody you're angry at.

Assuming you're angry at your accomplice, find sound ways of working out that inclination and let it go. This might be as basic a fix as talking over circumstances as they emerge that irritated you.

In certain cases, this might need the help of a therapist or middle person.

Try not to counterfeit it

Now and again it could feel simpler to counterfeit a orgasm or your longing as opposed to working out why it didn't work for you this time.

You might need to try not to make your accomplice feel awful. You may likewise simply need to get it over with on the off chance that you're depleted or can't stop your mind.

Be that as it may, this can be inconvenient to both your closeness and your capacity to further develop your sexual experiences together.

Speaking the truth about your sexual involvement with your accomplice can cause you to feel helpless, exposed, or humiliated. It is, in any case, an effective method for getting the discussion rolling about your sexual necessities so they can be tended to and met.

Try not to hold back on foreplay

In films, two individuals might eye each other across a jam-packed room and be prepared for sex with just one rushed, but energetic, kiss.

In actuality, it seldom works that way. Foreplay is much of the time an indispensable piece of preparing for different sorts of sex.

The sort of foreplay you take part in is additionally significant. Assist your partner with realizing where you like to be kissed and the way in which you like to be touched. Discuss what arouses both of you. Give a lot of it prior to continuing on toward the next stages.

Try not to hold back on afterplay

The time you spend together after you engage in sexual relations is significant, as well.

Assuming you promptly nod off or leap up and away from your accomplice subsequent to engaging in sexual relations, you're missing out on a chance to draw nearer to one another and manufacture more noteworthy degrees of closeness.

Talking, cuddling, or holding each other after sex is a way you approve your relationship and let your accomplice in on how they mean quite a lot to you.

This kind of closeness is significant for your relationship and for one another's confidence. It additionally helps set up for better, more associated sex from now on.

Get in a state of harmony about timing

Nobody's sex life stays static. In the beginning phases of your relationship, you might have intercourse a few times each day or week. Later on, how frequently you engage in sexual relations might reduce for some reasons, including the expansion of kids into your life, stress, and scheduling.

Libido additionally changes with time. Planning sex might seem like a turn off, yet for some couples, it sets a system they can rely on and anticipate.

You genuinely must lay out a timetable you both consent to. This might require reprioritizing different undertakings in your day to day activity and setting them aside for one another. It might likewise require compromise on the off chance that one of you wishes to engage in sexual relations more frequently than the other.

Booking sex likewise decreases the apprehensions about having one of you over and over turned down the other when not in that frame of mind.

Set the stage day in and day out

Assuming that sex is on your plan for the night, develop each other's expectation and want during the day. You can do this by sending each other hot messages or photographs. Consider sharing passages from a sexually explicit novel you both appreciate.

Develop your own feeling of expectation and excitement by allowing your mind to meander to the late evening's impending activities, as well.

Analyze

There's a huge swathe of sexual exercises you might explore as a team, giving that both of you are agreeable. These can incorporate everything from the utilization of toys and erotica to subjugation sex, tantric sex, and that's just the beginning.

Tense or unusual sex isn't, be that as it may, the way to cheerful sexual coexistence. Stirring it up can be just about as straightforward as wearing various sorts of dress or picking new areas to have intercourse.

It might likewise incorporate the use of new positions and kinds of sex, like oral sex, shared masturbation, and anal sex.

Trying different things with better approaches to give you both delight can be a great experiment in a couple's closeness, giving that you examine and settle on the things you'll attempt.

Address wellbeing worries that may be harming your sexual coexistence

As individuals age, real changes might make sex agonizing or troublesome.

Menopause might cause vaginal atrophy and dryness. Changes in hormonal levels can include decreases for testosterone production. This can diminish sexual longing and cause erectile dysfunction.

Medications might lessen drive or make it harder to climax.

Assuming that you're experiencing issues with sex that are related with an ailment, converse with your accomplice and to your doctor.

Advantages of having a cheerful sexual coexistence

Sexual fulfillment has been connected to various medical advantages. The sort of sex you have may influence the advantages you get. Here are only a few of the advantages:

- o Dealing with your sexual life can expand sensations of want and further develop drive.
- o Sex discharges feel-great chemicals like endorphins, assisting with lightening stress.

- A blissful sexual coexistence can extend your sensations of closeness with your accomplice.
- Individuals who appreciate sex with their accomplice experience expanded bliss and more fulfillments in life.
- Sex is a type of exercise and can work on cardiovascular well-being.
- Vaginal sex expands the flow of blood to the vagina, decreasing vaginal atrophy.
- Vaginal sex can likewise assist with fortifying vaginal muscles, lessening pelvic floor dysfunction.
- The incessant discharge might assist with forestalling prostate cancer.

CHAPTER 5

Sex Treatment: What You Ought to Be Aware

What is sex treatment?

Sex treatment is a kind of talk treatment that is intended to assist people and couples with tending to clinical, mental, personal, or interpersonal variables influencing sexual fulfillment.

The objective of sex treatment is to assist people move past physical and emotional difficulties to have a fantastic relationship and pleasurable sexual coexistence.

Sexual brokenness is normal. As a matter of fact, 43% of ladies and 31% of men report encountering sexual brokenness during their lifetimes of some sort. These dysfunctions might include:

- o Erectile brokenness
- o Low drive
- o Indifference
- o Untimely discharge

- o Low certainty
- o Absence of reaction to sexual boost
- o Failure to arrive at climax
- o Exorbitant charisma
- o Lack of sexual control
- o Troubling sexual thoughts
- o Undesirable sexual obsessions

Satisfying sexual coexistence is healthy and natural. Physical and emotional closeness are fundamental pieces of your well-being. At the point when sexual brokenness happens, having that satisfying sexual coexistence can be troublesome.

Sex treatment might help you reevaluate your sexual difficulties and increase your sexual fulfillment.

How really does sex treatment function?

Sex treatment resembles any sort of psychotherapy. You treat the condition by talking through your encounters, stresses, and feelings.

Along with your therapist, you then, at that point, figure out survival techniques to assist with working on your reactions in the future so you can have a better sexual life.

Your therapist will either converse with just you or with you and your accomplice at your initial appointments. The therapist is there to guide and assist you with handling your ongoing challenges:

- o They are not there to agree with one individual's stance or to assist with convincing anybody.
- o Additionally, everybody will keep their garments on. The sex advisor won't have sexual relations with anybody or tell anybody the best way to have intercourse.

With every meeting, your therapist will keep on pushing you toward better administration and acknowledgment of your interests that might be prompting sexual brokenness. All talk therapy, including sex therapy, is not just a supportive environment but also an educative environment too.

Giving solace and support to change is implied. You will probably have to leave your therapist's office with tasks and attempt to do them before your next appointment.

On the off chance that your therapist thinks the brokenness you're encountering is the consequence of actual sexual concern, they might allude you to a medical doctor.

Your therapist and the doctor can counsel about your signs and side effects and work to assist with finding any actual worries that might be adding to more prominent sexual issues.

Do I really want sex treatment?

One method for deciding whether you really want to see a sex therapist rather than another sort of talk therapist is to investigate which parts of your life are the most impacted by how you feel at the present time.

On the off chance that your personal satisfaction and profound well-being are significantly impacted by your sexual brokenness, it's smart to see a sex therapist. In like manner, on the off chance that an absence of intimacy or trouble speaking with an accomplice leads to your most serious individual concern, a sex therapist is the spot to begin.

How would I find a sex therapist?

A confirmed sex therapist can be an authorized psychiatrist, psychologist, marriage and family therapist, or clinical social worker. These psychological well-being specialists go through broad extra preparation in human sexuality to be certified as an ensured sex therapist.

Begin your inquiry with the American Association of Sexuality Educators, Counselors, and Therapists (AASECT). This association is answerable for supervising clinical preparation for sexual well-being experts. They additionally oversee qualifications for these medical services suppliers.

A licensed and certified therapist can be found through AASECT.

You can likewise do a Google or Psychology Today search for therapist in your space or call your neighborhood medical clinic or community education office. A significant number of these associations will joyfully give data on sex therapist in their network.

You can likewise ask your insurance agency. They might be able to provide you with a rundown of the names of confirmed sex therapist. You can deal with the rundown until you find the sex therapist you want.

In the event that you'd like a more private suggestion, talk with your health care provider, gynecologist, or urologist. Many specialists have met and prescribed sex therapist to their patients consistently. They could possibly guide you toward a provider whose style intently lines up with your own.

You can likewise converse with your companions. Raising personal subtleties can be challenging for certain individuals, however, in the event that you're open to asking a companion, they might have the option to suggest a specialist you and your accomplice can trust.

What to be aware of before seeing a therapist

At the point when you're prepared to start sex treatment, know these five things as you plan to settle on whom to meet for treatment.

Similarity

Therapists are one of a kind. Fruitful therapy really relies on how well you speak with your therapist and the amount you trust them and their direction to help you through your interests.

In the event that you feel awkward with a sex therapist anytime, search for another.

Solo versus couple

You don't need to carry your spouse with you to sex treatment. For certain people, solo sex treatment is sufficient to address concerns. For other people, having the two individuals present during treatment might assist with further developing fulfillment and fabricating a more grounded association.

Consult with your accomplice about your decision to start treatment. On the off chance that you'd like them to be involved, inquire.

Coordinated operations

While settling on a sex therapist, it's vital to consider where your therapist's office is and how accessible it is for you as you might be going for appointments during your lunch break, after work, or on irregular days when you have a free hour.

A few therapist likewise offer telehealth meetings, so you might have the option to meet with them online from the solace of your home.

Ensure it's advantageous to arrive at your doctor's office, or you might end up making reasons to stay away from it.

Treatment plan

Your therapist will probably go over an underlying treatment plan with you, during your first meetings. For most people and couples, a few meetings are expected from the start.

Nonetheless, when treatment is having a tremendous effect and your therapist feels certain you can deal with future difficulties, you might be set free from your therapist care.

Protection inclusion

Few out of every odd kind of health care coverage will cover psychotherapy. Those that truly do cover it might have extraordinary necessities or a individual deductible.

Affirm your insurance details with your insurance agency before you go for your appointment so you can be ready for the monetary investment.

The primary concern

A satisfying sexual coexistence is fundamental to your well-being for some reasons. Physical and emotional components of a solid sexual life have extensive advantages, including lower pulse, better heart wellbeing, and stress decrease. Sex is likewise only a natural, fun piece of life.

In any case, for certain individuals, sex is a wellspring of extraordinary uneasiness and stress. Sexual brokenness can prompt relationship entanglements, loss of certainty, and numerous other negative consequences.

Sex treatment is an integrative way to deal with treating and taking out basic difficulties. These worries might be physical, like low circulation. They may likewise be mental worries, like tension, stress, and certainty issues.

Sex treatment can assist people and couples with figuring out how to have open, genuine communication so they can manage any worries or difficulties toward a sound, happy sexual coexistence.

CHAPTER 6

The Most Effective Method to Up Your Relationship Closeness with Pillow Talk

At any point, do you take a gander at your accomplice and feel detached both physically and emotionally? We as a whole know that building a connection requires some time and effort. It likewise requires a readiness to be vulnerable and open to one another.

With our lives being loaded with perpetual daily agendas, work obligations, and family obligations, you may be considering the way in which you should cut out time in your timetable to work on your relationship. I have two words for you: Pillow Talk.

What is pillow talk?

Pillow Talk is a private, legitimate, unguarded discussion that happens between two sweethearts,

This kind of protected, adoring, certified association and conversation for the most part happens in bed or while snuggling. It likewise may occur previously or after sex with an accomplice, however, sex doesn't need to be important for the situation.

These discussions frequently don't include eye-to-eye connection, which permits you to talk all the more unknowingly, ignorant about the nonverbal signals of your accomplice. One reason pillow talk works, is on the grounds that it considers more inside and out discussions without self-control.

For certain individuals, this kind of discussion could happen normally, yet for other people, it very well may be harder to open up. I'll give some direction on the most proficient method to get the discussion — and closeness — streaming.

Pillow talks as opposed to speaking profanely

While speaking profanely during foreplay and sex can prompt an increased encounter and more personal time with your accomplice, it's not exactly the same thing as pillow talk. Pillow talk is all the more emotionally intimate and vulnerable.

You'll experience pillow talk most frequently previously or after sex when you and your accomplice are loose and agreeable. The focal point of pillow talk is on sure and elevating communication that brings individuals closer.

"It's considerably more about upgrading emotional intimacy and establishing a protected environment, which can improve sex too," she adds. When the two accomplices have a real sense of reassurance, comprehended, and associated, sex turns out to be seriously cherishing, and better, overall. In spite of the fact that it tends to be exotic or in light of sexuality, pillow talk doesn't happen during sex.

Speaking profanely is completely used to improve sexual activity and is much of the time more express and physically charged and invigorating. Speaking profanely can improve the act of sex, if and when the two accomplices are agreeable and stimulated by it.

How can pillow talk help your relationship?

On the off chance that your sex life doesn't appear as though it's going on pretty fine lately, you may be contemplating whether pillow talk can assist with helping boost your activity in the bedroom. The short response is true, it can.

Pillow talk eventually causes the two accomplices to feel like they can put their guard down and feel nearer, which increases love for one another as well as confidence.

Since most pillow talk happens while you're resting, loose, and cuddling, it's not unexpected to encounter an expansion in oxytocin, the bonding love hormone. This hormone normally helps two individuals feel close and connected and helps cultivate sensations of being infatuated.

Eventually, pillow talk helps settles a relationship. It very well may be the extension between casual sex and falling head over heels, since our emotional connection eventually causes a couple to stay together and to feel affection for one another.

In any case, it's not only the before-sex pillow talk that upgrades a relationship: What you do and say after issues similarly to such an extent, while possibly not more. As a matter of fact, a recent report showed that cuddling, talking, and stroking all add to more readily sex and a higher rating of relationship fulfillment.

Instances of pillow talk

Still not certain what constitute pillow talk? Here are a few models that you and your accomplice can use at beginning stages:

- o Discussing what you love about one another
- o Sharing dreams for the future, travel, and experience, and things you need to attempt as a team
- o Reviewing exceptional moments, similar to when you originally fell head over heels
- o Discussing fears that need soothing
- o Reminding each other how much you love each other
- o Sharing good credits and signals that can assist you to collaborate with feeling more secure and surer
- o Perceiving the significance of things from before

The most effective method to begin

To begin, couples need to at times make arrangements for these things. I frequently recommend an arranged discussion for 10 minutes, where you can't discuss issues with your relationship, your work, your friends (or their relationships), kids, other relatives, governmental issues, social media, and so on.

This is to be a chance to return to who you used to be and sort out what moved you, what took care of you, and what you tried for as a team.

In spite of the fact that closeness can be unnerving for certain individuals, particularly in the underlying phases of a relationship, it's the main way we keep up with enduring relationships. Ways to help are to:

a. Touch
b. Gaze into each other's eyes
c. Embrace
d. Giggle
e. Reassure your partner

Likewise, revealing our own insecurities can be an extraordinary method for starting.

Alternate ways of feeling close

Despite the fact that pillow talk can do astounding things for a relationship, it's likewise really smart to have different devices to stir up the fire.

- o Invest more energy in touching one another. Touching your accomplice can set off emotional wellbeing and consider greater vulnerability.
- o No electronic gadgets in the bed. Cell phones and the capacity to stream live 24 hours daily aren't helping our love lives. As opposed to heading to sleep with your telephone for entertainment, why not grab your accomplice instead.
- o Back rubs can likewise be great. Couples massage is an extraordinary method for uniting you.
- o Clasping hands. Something as basic as clasping hands can have a major effect on the way you feel about one another.
- o Communicating your requirements. Investing energy in discussing what you like or need to attempt sexually can assist you with feeling nearer as a couple. This incorporates paying attention to our accomplices and attempting new things outside the bedroom also.

o Talking about your thoughts. Making a place of refuge for yourself as well as your accomplice to communicate feelings is a definitive articulation of profound closeness.

Solid sex tips for men

Sex is a psychological and actual pursuit that occasionally feels like it ought to have come with an instruction guide. Likewise, with whatever else, one man's preferences could be very not quite the same as another preference. It tends to be a task to find the right fixings to an associated and orgasmic sexual coexistence.

As a man, it's vital to take part in exercises that will keep you up with your general well-being, which plays into your sexual well-being. Decreasing pressure, eating right, working out, and staying away from unfortunate behavior patterns like smoking and savoring liquor abundance can keep you in prime shape. A sound way of life likewise gives you sexual certainty, which is definitely not a bad side effect. At the point when you have the psychological side of your sex game in gear, you can zero in on the actual side.

Sound sex "do's"

Sex doesn't need to resemble films to be perfect. It's among you and your accomplice to figure out what turns both of you on and what interfaces you two. Here are a few hints to assist you with taking sex to a higher level.

Dominating foreplay

With regard to foreplay, the key "triggers" for individuals can appear to be altogether different. For instance, if you inquire as to whether your spouse needs to have intercourse and she rapidly says no, you could be posing the right inquiry with the wrong words or body language.

Foreplay is about the inclination and needs. It's essential to show that you would simply prefer not just to have intercourse, but that you need to have intercourse with your accomplice, specifically.

Solid sex "don'ts"

During sex; Now and again the most significant don'ts with regards to sex are the easiest to say and the most challenging to grasp. However, science and dependable information make a large portion of these activities major don'ts with regards to sex:

- o **Rushing sex or behaving like it's an errand**. This is particularly evident assuming that you're controlling everything giving your accomplice oral sex or other excitement. Sex is about bliss and taking time.
- o **Anticipating appreciation or response**. While a ton of times you can hope to give and get, requesting it is a seriously unique thing. You shouldn't expect acclaim each time you participate in foreplay (regardless of whether you need to or did a particularly extraordinary work). Get things done in the bedroom because you need to, not on the grounds that you have to or in light of the fact that you anticipate a great deal of much obliged.

Other significant don'ts to be aware

A significant don't for sex is zeroing in on the final product and not on the process. Other don'ts to note include:

- o Having harsh sex or play without conversing with your accomplice. Safe words that can demonstrate when you've gone excessively far exist on purpose. Lay out one assuming the line is crossed between joy and agony.

- o Giving interruptions access. No messaging, phone call, or halting to really look at the score of a game.
- o Calling your accomplice by another name. This one justifies itself with real evidence.
- o Remaining totally quiet. From groans to inspirational statements, telling your accomplice you're into it can go quite far.

10 different ways how to discuss sex with your accomplice

All in all, how to discuss sex with your accomplice? How to begin a sex discussion?

Assuming that discussing sex with your accomplice concerns you, there are multiple ways how to discuss sex with your accomplice effectively (seriously!):

a. Just do it

This is a scandalous trademark of a renowned sport brand, which, truly, is an incredible rallying call.

Pushing for a real discussion, and simply going with it, may be valued by your accomplice.

Who can say for sure, all it could take is one straight-to-the-point discussion to fire up things in the bedroom.

b. Put it in a positive light and offer thanks

Individuals like being valued overall. A strategy that could be utilized in communicating your sexual need is to try communicating these necessities by placing them in a more positive light.

Rather than saying: "Might you at any point do X more regularly?"

Have a go at expressing it thusly: "I love it when you do X. I feel a debt of gratitude to such an extent."

In the event that you look at the two assertions, there is a notable shift in regard to the energy that you are attempting to put out.

The best thing about the second statement is that you are additionally offering thanks for something that your accomplice is doing for you as opposed to offering hidden criticism.

Studies have shown that being valued in a relationship is very much appreciated and advances a trusting and solid relationship.

Among its advantages is that the great deed is supported and is repeated even the more.

Look at these three degrees of appreciation and how they can further develop relationships:

c. Get it on paper

Assuming you're the sort of accomplice who is more powerful while conveying a message by means of writing you'll likely find this approach a lot simpler. However, assuming you're doing it along these lines, ensure that you're conveying it clearly.

d. Get a clear line of sight with a sharing time

One of the ways how to discuss sex with your accomplice is to get visual.

A few accomplices utilize a little pornography, whether in books or in videos, to pass on what they need to do. In any case, take caution, as excessively porn could become counterproductive for your relationship.

e. "I" proclamations

"I" proclamations have many advantages with regard to how to discuss sex with your accomplice.

"I" proclamations when couples are discussing sex permit the couple to express their genuine thoughts with next to no coercion or wavering. It likewise assists accomplices with seeing each other's particular issues with practically no questions and miscommunication. Plus, it forestalls an attempt at finger-pointing in the relationship.

f. Examine how to say No

There ought not to be any intricacies while expressing No to sex. Sex ought to absolutely be about assent with no space for pressurizing, guilt, manipulation, and coercion.

Along these lines, sex discussions between couples ought to be clear and direct where you both let each other know you're not prepared.

g. Try not to assume gender roles

Talking about sex turns a great deal simpler when you both try not to assume what the other partner endlessly shouldn't do. In the event that you feel the other partner ought to continuously start sex or they ought to act a specific way, you really want to work on that.

These stem a ton from the assumptions you could have from your accomplice. Convey them as opposed to assuming.

h. Do it brilliantly

There's generally an ideal opportunity and some unacceptable chance to make the discussion.

Ensure you pick the right moment to talk about sex. For example, it ought to not be in that time of the day when both of you are occupied with your errands. Pick the right time and guarantee your accomplice is free too before you start the discussion.

i. Show compassion

While you and your accomplice talk sex, ensure you are empathetic and grasp their interests and wants. Try not to act unempathetic. You are on this journey together, and being benevolent to one another in the process is fundamental.

j. Grasp the distinctions

There could be countless things different between you and your accomplice. Along these lines, instead of responding adversely to sexual conversation starters, realize that differing on specific parts of sex is alright. You both simply should be open to one another's considerations and needs.

What to do when your accomplice would rather not pay attention to you

Examining one's sexual necessities is fundamental in any relationship, regardless of whether you're married or not. All in all, what do you do in the event that your accomplice decides not to pay attention to you?

A famous love citation says, "It is smarter to have loved and lost than never to have loved."

Of course, you've given a valiant effort to impart and convey your requirements in a way that would have ensured a positive outcome; however on the off chance that your accomplice decides not to pay attention to you, perhaps it's time to bring in the fortifications of a sex therapist.

It is additionally vital to expect that not all dreams will be generally welcomed by our accomplices. All things considered, we're different individuals, and we will undoubtedly have different cravings and needs.

Calling a sex therapist or a counselor could be useful in conveying even the most sensitive of issues.

CONCLUSION

Promising to invest more energy participated in pillow talks with your accomplice can assist with helping your relationship, bring you closer, and establish an environment that encourages intimacy. Besides, it's something you can deal with together, and the more you make it happen, the simpler it will be.

A blissful sexual coexistence takes communication and work. Sexual fulfillment is one method for expanding the general happiness in life. It likewise assists couples with remaining connected emotionally.

Recollect that the two players ought to excitedly agree to have intercourse. Since you are having sexual relations with your drawn-out accomplice doesn't mean assent has been given.

Assuming you at any point feel physically pressured by an accomplice, compelled to engage in sexual relations, or be touched in a way you would rather not, do know that your healthcare providers are consistently prepared to help you.

You can converse with your doctor or a social specialist about any worries you have.